1. Introduction

Government bodies often hold procurement auctions for multiple projects simultaneously. For example, state and local governments often hold simultaneous auctions for one-year contracts to supply milk, bread and other goods to proximate school districts and prisons. Multiple simultaneous auctions are common for contracts to build roads. If the firms bidding in the auction had constant marginal cost, the fact that multiple projects are bid upon simultaneously would be largely irrelevant. However, when the bidders face increasing costs of additional projects their bidding strategies become more complex. Moreover, under these circumstances there is a coordination problem: While total production cost may be minimized by an even distribution of projects across bidders, this allocation is unlikely to be achieved in a symmetric equilibrium.

This paper presents a model of bidding for multiple projects under increasing cost. The model, I assumes that there are two bidders for two identical projects to be purchased by a buyer at auction.[1] The two buyers have ex-ante identical costs (which may differ ex-post) and face increasing incremental production costs. Under these circumstances, the coordination problem discussed above may arise. For example, if a symmetric pure-strategy equilibrium emerges, small differences in realized cost will lead to one bidder winning both bids.

The coordination problem can be ameliorated if bidders have asymmetric bidding strategies whereby one bidder has a common price across auctions, while the other bidder bids "high" sometimes and "low" sometimes.[2] This will result in each bidder winning half the bids more frequently than in the symmetric equilibrium. Moreover, these bids represent a non cooperative equilibrium. If bidder j bids a common price on all projects, i's optimal (non cooperative) reaction is not to bid the same amount on all projects. Rather i will bid low enough to win some bids, but will not find it in its interest to bid below j everywhere. That is, by bidding 'low' on some projects, and 'high' on others, i guarantees itself some share of the projects, but is able to avoid the potential for winning so many bids that it loses money. Given this strategy by i, j finds that a strategy of bidding the same price everywhere serves to guarantee itself some share of the projects.

---

[1] Government procurement auctions frequently have only two participants.

[2] Figure 1 details the actual bids made by the two bidders in four simultaneous auctions. This paper in part represents an attempt to explain this behavior.

The existence of this non cooperative equilibrium is interesting for several reasons. First, it provides an explanation of actual bidding behavior is a series of simultaneous auctions (see Figure 1). Second, to the extent that this equilibrium emerges it explains why government agencies hold auctions simultaneously, even though sequential auctions mitigate the coordination problem. As I show, while sequential auctions lead to lower total production costs, they lead to higher winning bids.

Finally, government agencies have begun to examine pricing behavior in order to spot "patterns" which suggest the existence of bid-rigging. This approach has been advocated by some economists as well. For example, Rothrock et al. (1978) suggest that descriptive statistics can help identify markets in which collusion has occured.[3] The existance of an asymmetric equilibrium under fairly general conditions suggests such an approach may be counterproductive. Determining if collusion occured by observing prices requires the investigator to know the non cooperative equilibrium.[4] Even with the simplest type of cost interdependency (i.e., increasing cost) across projects, the non cooperative equilibrium may appear collusive.[5] When cost interdepencies are more complicated (e.g., optimal routing of delivery trucks, lumpiness in production facilities), the equilibrium may take a different seemingly-collusive form.

2. EQUILIBRIUM AUCTION STRATEGIES UNDER INCREASING COSTS

A. A Model of Auctions Under Increasing Costs

To formalize the structure described above, let the production cost of player k ($k = i,j$) be

$c_1 + e_k$ if one project is produced and

$c_1 + c_2 + 2e_k$ if two projects are produced

where $c_2 > c_1$, and e_k, a random component of costs, is uniformly distributed with support $[0,\bar{e}]$ where the

---

[3]They suggest that too little variability of bids could imply agreements among firms (at 25).

[4]Kendricks and Porter (1989) suggest ways in which collusive behavior may be identified, but note that these tests depend on knowing the nature of the collusive activity.

[5] For example, if bidder j indicates its intention to bid a common price on each of a series of auctions, bidder i could then shade j's by a small amount in one-half the auctions, while bidding well above j's price on the other half. This would result in collusively high prices, with a minimum amount of communication. The pattern of bids which emerges resembles the non cooperative asymmetric equilibrium described above.

realizations of e_i and e_j are independent.[6] Thus, each bidder knows its own realization of e_t, but views its rival's cost as a random variable, so that the model is an independent values auction.

On the buyers' side of the market, I assume that there is a risk-neutral buyer with two identical projects.[7] The buyer establishes first-price sealed-bid auctions to choose among suppliers. The question for the buyer implicitly analyzed in this paper is whether to hold these auctions simultaneously or sequentially.[8]

From the social perspective, the basic allocation problem is that given costs which increase with output, total production costs will (generally) be minimized by having each seller produce one project. If buyers use simultaneous auctions, small differences in realized costs could result in one seller winning both bids. For example, suppose that bids were to be entered simultaneously for two projects. If the two bidders have identical strategies that result in a symmetric equilibrium in pure strategies, the probability that one would win both is at least one half.[9]

One situation in which the coordination problem may well emerge is where several proximate municipalities invite bids for supplying some product to schools. Generally, the bidding is held in the spring for the following school year, and winners are announced weeks or months after the auction. Hence, bidders often do not know the outcome of previous auctions when making a bid. In one specific instance which came

---

[6] This last assumption is not restrictive in that for a more general specification, the correlated element of the error term can be incorporated into the c_1 and c_2 terms. That is, e_t is the firm-specific element of costs.

[7] Equivalently, there might be two buyers with identical projects.

[8] If the buyer's side of the market consists of two identical firms, the analogous question is, given the auction date selected by buyer 1, should buyer 2 hold an auction prior to that date, after that date, or simultaneously with buyer 1's auction. Note that simultaneously need not mean literally on the same date, but simply that bidders on buyer 2's project do not know the outcome of the bidding on the buyer 1's project when they make bids on buyer 2's project.

[9] If the two projects were for the same buyer, the buyer could avoid this problem by having each seller submit a schedule of bids (e.g., one price for completing one project, another price for completing both). While using this auction mechanism (which Bernheim and Whinston (1986) refer to as a "menu auction") eliminates the social cost problem, it may result in higher prices than either of the two equilibrium derived in this paper. Specifically, applying the results in Anton and Yao (1989 - Lemma 1), the equilibrium total price for the two projects will be at least $c_1 + c_2 + 2 \max(e_i, e_j)$, which can be greater (in expected value) than the prices derived below. In this paper however, I consider circumstances under which holding menu auctions is not feasible or desirable (as would be the case if each project is for a different municipality).

3

to trial,[10] several Baltimore-area school districts held simultanous auctions to purchase milk for the following school year. The Department of Justice noted the potential coordination problem in its brief "[a]ny dairy might hope to win any given bid, but the range of prices competition was likely to produce was narrow enough that a small difference in price might bring about far more business than it could efficiently handle. Moreover, the cost calculations on which a competitive bid depended contained assumptions about volume of milk processed, over-all volume of half-pint containers processed, and volume of school milk obtained. It was easy to miscalculate. No dairy, not even Sealtest as it turned out, could handle [all] the school business profitably".[11]

This illustrates the basic difficulty with simultaneous auctions under increasing costs. One way to mitigate (but not eliminate, as shown in section 3) the coordination problem is to hold the auction sequentially. With sequential auctions, in the second auction vendors would know whether they won the first auction, and hence they would know their costs of fulfilling the contract prior to bidding. While this does reduce expected production costs relative to a simultaneous auction, it will tend to result in higher prices than a simultaneous auction.

The above discussion of the simultaneous auction was based on a pure-strategy symmetric equilibrium emerging. Of course, a pure-strategy symmetric equilibrium need not be the only equilibrium in a simultaneous auction (indeed, it may not even be an equilibrium). In part B of this section, I derive an asymmetric equilibrium for the simultaneous auction. In that equilibrium the social allocation problem will be mitigated, relative to the symmetric auction. To see how asymmetric strategies can ameliorate the coordination problem, suppose bidder i knows that bidder j bid the same price in each of q^* auctions, although i is uncertain as to the level of that bid. Specifically, suppose that j's bid on all of the projects to be auctioned (b_j) is known to be distributed on (b^j_{min}, b^j_{max}) as in figure 2. Then, by making bids according to schedule b_i in figure 2, i can guarantee itself at least q^i_{min} number of winning bids, and no more than q^i_{max}. Similarly, suppose j knows the shape of i's bid function, but does not know where the function lies on the interval

---

[10] U.S. v. Koontz Creamery, Inc, 257 F. Supp. 1274 (1983) at 307.

[11] From Government's post-hearing brief, as cited by the court in Koontz.

(b^i_{min}, b^i_{max}) in figure 3.[12] By bidding b_j, j guarantees itself at least q^j_{min} and no more than q^j_{max}. Thus, the asymmetric strategies mitigate the coordination problem.

The remainder of this section derives the optimal strategy of each vendor, given the other vendor's strategy. That is, I assume that both vendors maintain Nash conjectures about its competitor's bidding strategy and derive the Nash equilibrium. Part B of this section derives the asymmetric equilibrium in the simultaneous auction. Part C derives the Nash equilibrium in the sequential auction, generalizing the above situation to allow for uncertainty. Section 3 compares prices and social costs under these two equilibria.

B. Asymmetric Equilibrium in Simultaneous Auctions

In this section, I derive an asymmetric equilibrium to the auction environment described above. Lemma 1 shows that if player j makes the same bid on both projects, and those bids are linear functions of e_j, then i's optimal response is to bid "high" on one project, and "low" on the other. Lemma 2 shows the converse; if i's bids are two distinct linear functions of e_i (over some relevant range), then j's optimal response is to bid the same amount on both projects. Hence, there exists an asymmetric Nash equilibrium in pure strategies. Proposition 1 explicitly solves for the equilibrium bid functions.

The intuition is the same as that illustrated in figures 2 and 3: i's strategy insures that it wins one bid "most" of the time, and wins both bids only at a price above his costs of completing the second project. Given i's strategy, bidding the same amount on the two projects accomplishes the same thing for bidder j.

Define b_1^i as player i's bids on project 1, using similar notation for the i's bid on project 2, and j's bids on the two projects. Let $P(W,L)$ be the probability that player i wins the first bid and loses the second (i.e., $b_1^i < b_1^j$ and $b_2^i > b_2^j$). Using the same notation for all relevant probabilities, we can write player i's maximand as

(1) $\pi = (b_1^i - c_1 - e_i) P(W,L) + (b_2^i - c_1 - e_i) P(L,W) + (b_1^i + b_2^i - c_1 - c_2 - 2e_i) P(W,W)$.

---

[12]The downward slope of b_j in figure 3 represents the same bidding strategy as the upward sloping function in figure 2. The difference is that in figure 2 the horizontal axis is the number of projects awarded to bidder i, while the horizontal axis in figure 3 is the number awarded to bidder j (= q^* - the number won by bidder i).

<u>Lemma 1</u>: Let player j bid the same amount on the two projects, where j's bid is a linear function of e_j (Hence, from i's perspective, j's bids are uniformly distributed on $(b^j(0), b^j(\bar{e}))$). Then i's optimal bids are

(2) $b_1^i = (c_1 + e_i + b^j(\bar{e}))/2$ if $e_i \geq 2b^j(0) - c_1 - b^j(\bar{e}) \equiv \hat{e}$

   $= b^j(0)$ if $e_i \leq \hat{e}$

(3) $b_2^i = (c_2 + e_i + b^j(\bar{e}))/2$

<u>Proof</u>: See Appendix

Note that $\partial b_2^i/\partial e_i = 1/2$ and $\partial b_1^i/\partial e_i = 1/2$ for $e_i > 2b^j(0) - c_1 - b^j(\bar{e})$, and over that range both bids are uniformly distributed, with $b_2^i - b_1^i = (c_2 - c_1)/2 \equiv \Delta c/2 > 0$.[13] Also note that an analogous result holds for any number of projects, as long as j bids the same amount on all projects.

Given this strategy by i, consider j's optimal reaction. Bidder j maximizes the objective function in equation 4,

(4) $\pi = (b_1^j - c_1 - e^j) P(W,L) + (b_2^j - c_1 - e^j) P(L,W) + (b_1^j + b_2^j - c_1 - c_2 - 2 e^j) P(W,W)$.

It is useful to note that while j's objective function resembles that of bidder i, the probabilities are somewhat more complex. In particular the lower of the two bids facing j (i.e., made by i), which I denote b_L^i, is distributed uniformly on $[(c_1 + b^j(\bar{e}))/2, (c_1 + \hat{e} + b^j(\bar{e}))/2]$ for $e_i > 2b^j(0) - c_1 - b^j(\bar{e}) (\equiv \hat{e})$, while the higher of the two bids (b_H^i) is distributed uniformly on $[(c_2 + b^j(\bar{e}))/2, (c_2 + \hat{e} + b^j(\bar{e}))/2]$. Thus, the probability of j winning the bid on the first project but the losing the second will depend upon which project represents i's lower bid.

<u>Lemma 2</u>: Let player i bid as in equations 2 and 3. Then j's optimal bid is the same amount on both projects. Specifically, j's optimal bids are

(5) $b_1^j = b_2^j = (c_1 + c_2)/4 + e_j/2 + (b_H^i(\hat{e}) + 2b_L^i(\hat{e}))/6$

---

[13] For values of e_i such that $c_2 + e_i > b^j(\bar{e})$, the constraint that $b^j(\bar{e}) \geq b_2^i$ is binding so that no interior solution exists. However, for values of e_i such that $b^j(\bar{e}) < c_2 + e_i$ there is no alternative bid by i which would result in higher profit than the strategy in equation 3, since any winning bid would be at a price below cost. Hence, the strategy in (3) is weakly dominant everywhere.

for $\tilde{e} < 4\Delta c/3$.

Proof: See Appendix

Lemmas 1 and 2 demonstrate that firms may have asymmetric strategies even when the firms have identical costs and act simultaneously. Given the bidding strategies in Lemmas 1 and 2, it is possible to explicit solve for the equilibrium strategies. The equilibrium bid functions are derived in Proposition 1 and depicted in Figure 4.

Proposition 1: If the auctions for two projects are held simultaneously, then an asymmetric Nash equilibrium exists of the form

7. A. $b^j(e_j) = (c_2 + c_1)/2 + 3\tilde{e}/8 + e_j/2$

   B. $b_L^i(e_i) = (c_2 + 3c_1)/4 + 7\tilde{e}/16 + e_i/2$

   C. $b_H^i(e_i) = (3c_2 + c_1)/4 + 7\tilde{e}/16 + e_i/2$

   D. $\hat{e} = \Delta c/2 - \tilde{e}/8$

for $4\Delta c/9 \leq \tilde{e} \leq 4\Delta c/3$.

Proof: Lemma 1 shows that equations 2 and 3 are best-response functions for player i, while Lemma 2 shows that equation 5 is j's best-response function. Combining these three equations with the identity which defines $\hat{e}$ constitute 4 equations in 4 unknowns ($\hat{e}$, $b_H^i(\hat{e})$, $2b_L^i(\tilde{e})$, $b_j(\tilde{e})$). Solving these simultaneously yields

$b^j(e_j) = (c_2 + c_1)/2 + 7\tilde{e}/8$

$b_L^i(\tilde{e}) = (c_2 + 3c_1)/4 + 15\tilde{e}/16$

$b_H^i(\hat{e}) = c_2 + 3\tilde{e}/8$

$\hat{e} = \Delta c/2 - \tilde{e}/8$.

Since $\hat{e}$ must be less than $\tilde{e}$, a necessary condition for this to be an equilibrium is $\Delta c/2 - \tilde{e}/8 < \tilde{e}$, or $\tilde{e} > 4\Delta c/9$. Using the fact that $\partial b^j(e_j)/\partial e_j = \partial b_L^i(e_i)/\partial e_i = \partial b_H^i(e_i)/\partial e_i = 1/2$, for $e_i > \hat{e}$

7. A. $b^j(e_j) = (c_2 + c_1)/2 + 3\bar{e}/8 + e_j/2$

   B. $b_L^i(e_i) = (c_2 + 3c_1)/4 + 7\bar{e}/16 + e_i/2$

   C. $b_H^i(e_i) = (3c_2 + c_1)/4 + 7\bar{e}/16 + e_i/2$

   D. $\hat{e} = \Delta c/2 - \bar{e}/8$.

From the proof of Lemma 2, we know that a condition for this equilibrium to exist is that j does not have the incentive to bid below $b_L^i(\hat{e})$ (and win both bids for all e_i). The gain to j from shading is

$$\frac{\hat{e}}{\bar{e}}(b_L^i(\hat{e})-c_2-e_j)-\frac{\bar{e}-\hat{e}}{\bar{e}}(b_j(e_j)-b_L^i(\hat{e}))-(b_j(e_j)-b_L^i(\hat{e}))$$

$$= \frac{1}{\bar{e}}[2\bar{e}(b_L^i(\hat{e})-b^j(e_j)) + \hat{e}\ (b^j(e_j)-c_2-e_j)]$$

Using (7), this has the same sign as

$$(8)\quad -(2\bar{e})\frac{e_j}{2}+\hat{e}(\frac{3\bar{e}}{8}-\frac{e_j}{2}-\frac{\Delta c}{2}) = -\frac{e_j}{2}(2\bar{e}+\hat{e})+(\frac{\Delta c}{2}-\frac{\bar{e}}{8})(\frac{3\bar{e}}{8}-\frac{\Delta c}{2})$$

Note that if $\bar{e} < 4\Delta c/3$, the expression in (8) is negative, implying that j does not have the incentive to shade. Hence, equations 7A-D constitute an equilibrium for $4\Delta c/3 \geq \bar{e} \geq 4\Delta c/9$. As equation 8 is decreasing in e_j, when $\bar{e} > 4\Delta c/3$, j will have the incentive to bid below $b_L^i(\hat{e})$ for e_j sufficiently small. ∎

Proposition 1 shows that an asymmetric equilibrium exists. The intuition behind the result can be seen most readily when costs are certain. Suppose bidder j bids the same amount on the two projects, and this common bid is b^j, where $c_2 > b^j > c_1$. Then bidder i can earn $b^j - c_1 - \alpha > 0$ (α arbitrarily small) by bidding $b^j - \alpha$ on one project and $b^j + \delta$ on the other ($\delta \in (\alpha, c_2 - b^j)$). It can be readily verified that i cannot improve on this strategy.

Similarly, suppose that i bids b_1^i, b_2^i where $c_2 > b_2^i > b_1^i > c_1$. Then bidder j's best strategy is to bid $b^j = b_2^i - \eta$ (η arbitrarily small) on both bids. Such a strategy guarantees a return of $b_2^i - c_1 - \eta > 0$. Here again, it can be readily verified that this strategy yields higher profit than any alternative.

The reason this equilibrium requires some degree of uncertainty follows from this heuristic. Under certainty, bidder i's optimal lower bid is arbitrarily close to j's bid, while j's optimal bid is arbitrarily close to i's higher bid. Hence, i's two bids are always arbitrarily close to one another, and there is no asymmetric equilibrium. For the asymmetric equilibrium to exist, there must be sufficient uncertainty (relative to the slope of the cost curves) so that each bidder may want to win both bids, given the other bidder's strategy.

C. Sequential Auctions

Given the potential coordination problem associated with simultaneous auctions, one might ask whether buyers might be better off holding the auctions sequentially, allowing the bidders to know whether they had won on the first bid prior to making a second bid.[14] While this solution does mitigate the problem of inefficient production, it may result in higher prices for the buyers. To see why, consider the sequential equilibrium under certainty, (i.e., where both bidder's costs are simply c_1 for the one project and $c_1 + c_2$ for two). Then the firm which lost the first auction will bid c_2 minus ϵ and earn a rent of $c_2 - \epsilon - c_1$ in the second auction. Of course, neither firm would bid less than $c_2 - \epsilon$ in the first auction because it would be better off losing. Hence the equilibrium bids will be $c_2 - \epsilon$ in both auctions. These exceed the maximum possible winning bids in the asymmetric equilibrium described in equation 7.

Formally, equilibrium to the sequential auction is obtained in a recursive manner, solving first for the second-auction solution (Propositions 2 and 3). The equilibrium in the second auction is derived under the assumption that a symmetric equilibrium obtains in the first auction. This means that the loser in the first auction (bidder i) knows that $e_i > e_j$. Bidders in the second auction are asymmetrically situated in a second sense as well by virtue of the outcome of the first auction. Bidder i knows that j's costs are $c_2 + e_j$ in the second auction, while its own are $c_1 + e_i$. For any realization of e, a bidder will know both conditional expected profits (i.e., those associated with either winning or losing the first auction) in the second auction. Bidders then calculate their first auction bids, treating the difference in expected profits as a cost of winning

---

[14] I assume that both auctions are conducted prior to any work on the projects, or payment by the buyer. Hence the only difference between simultaneous and sequential auctions is whether the seller knows the outcome of one auction prior to bidding on the second.

the first auction.

In general, the second-auction equilibrium bids will be functions of the degree of uncertainty, as measured by ē. When ē is 'small' (as detailed in Proposition 2), the equilibrium in the second-auction results in the first-auction loser winning the bid regardless of e_i and e_j. When uncertainty is 'small', the intuition of the certainty case is preserved. On the other hand when ē is not 'small', different equilibrium bid functions emerge, and either bidder can win the second auction.

Proposition 2: Let bidder j be the winner of the first auction. Then if ē < $\Delta c/2$, a second-auction equilibrium is

$b_j = c_2 + e_j$

$b_i = c_2$.

Proof: Let ē < $\Delta c/2$, and suppose that the first-auction winner (j) bids its costs ($c_2 + e_j$) in the second auction. Then bidder i chooses b_i to maximize

$(b_i - c_1 - e_i)$ Prob$(b_i < b_j)$.

Given that the bidders had identical bid functions in period 1 and j won, i knows that $e_j \leq e_i$. Hence, e_j is distributed uniformly on $(0, e_i)$, and if $e_i > b_i - c_2$.

$$Prob\ (b_i < b_j) = \int_{b_i}^{c_2 + e_i} f(b(e_j)) db(e_j) = \frac{1}{e_i} \cdot \int_{b_i - c_2}^{e_i} de_j = \frac{c_2 + e_i - b_i}{e_i}$$

Hence,

$\pi_i = (b_i - c_1 - e_i)(e_i + c_2 - b_i)/e_i + \lambda(b_i - c_2)$

$d\pi/db_i = (-2b_i + c_1 + e_i + e_i + c_2)/e_i + \lambda$.

Setting this equal to zero and solving yields

9) $b_i = (c_1 + c_2)/2 + e_i + \lambda/2$

10) $b_i \geq c_2$.

This constraint is binding for all e_i if ē < $\Delta c/2$, so that $b_i = c_2$ for $e_i \leq \Delta c/2$. Given this strategy by i, j cannot improve on a strategy of bidding $c_2 + e_j$. If j lowers its bid, it will bid below its costs and lose money, while increasing its bid yields the same (0) profit as $c_2 + e_j$. Hence, $b_j = c_2 + e_j$ is weakly dominant. ∎

These results imply that if $\Delta c/2 \geq \bar{e}$, bidder j never wins the second auction, and the incremental return to losing the first auction is simply $(c_2 - c_1 - e_i)$. Thus, if $\bar{e} \leq \Delta c/2$, there is a 'small' amount of uncertainty and, as in the certainty case, the first auction loser always wins the second auction.

If the amount of uncertainty is not 'small' (i.e., if $\bar{e} > \Delta c/2$) then i's optimal strategy will no longer be $b_i = c_2$ everywhere. To derive the Nash equilibrium for $\bar{e} > \Delta c/2$, it is convenient to define $\check{e}$ and $\hat{e}$.[15]

Definition 1: Let $\check{e}$ be the maximum value of e_i such that $b_i(\check{e}) = b_j(0)$.

Definition 2: Let $\hat{e}$ be the minimum value of e_j such that $c_2 + \hat{e} = b_i(\check{e})$.

If b_i is strictly increasing in e_i for $e_i \geq \check{e}$, then it follows that $b_i(e_i) > b_j(0)$ for all $e_i > \check{e}$. That is, for $e_i < \check{e}$ i bids $b_j(0)$ and wins with certainty, while for $e_i > \check{e}$ i's bid is the unconstrained optimum. Similarly, if $b_j(e_j)$ is strictly increasing in e_j, then whenever $e_j < \hat{e}$ j's bid is sufficiently low that there is a positive probability it will win (i.e., $b_j(e_j) < b_i(\check{e})$ for all $e_j < \hat{e}$).

Proposition 3: For $\bar{e} > \Delta c/2$, a second-auction equilibrium is

(11) $b_i = \quad (2c_1 + c_2)/3 + (3e_i + \bar{e})/4$ for $e_i \geq \check{e}$

$\qquad (c_1 + 2c_2)/3 + \bar{e}/2 \qquad$ for $e_i \leq \check{e}$

(12) $b_j = \quad (c_1 + 2c_2)/3 + (e_j + \bar{e})/2$

where $\check{e} = \bar{e}/3 + 4/9\Delta c$, $\hat{e} = \bar{e} - 2\Delta c/3$.

Proof: See Appendix.

Equations (11) and (12) imply that for $\bar{e} < 2\Delta c/3$, $\check{e}$ is greater than $\bar{e}$. Recalling definition 1, this

---

[15] These definitions hold for any arbitrary belief i(j) has about j's (i's) bid function. That is, j takes $\bar{e}$ as given when choosing its optimal bid. Only in equilibrium does j's perception of i's bid function necessarily match i's actual bid function.

means that i bids $(c_1 + 2c_2)/3 + \varepsilon/2$ everywhere, and always wins the second auction.

Propositions 2 and 3 detail the second period equilibrium. Given this equilibrium in the second auction, consider the first-auction equilibrium. In order to induce one of the bidders to win the first auction, the equilibrium in the first auction must result in returns which equal or exceed the return to losing. Let $\pi_2(e_i)$ represent the differential second auction profit associated with losing the first auction. As noted above, if $\varepsilon < 2\Delta c/3$ the first-auction loser always wins the second auction and $\pi_2(e_i)$ is equal to second-auction profits. If $\varepsilon < \Delta c/2$, the winning price is c_2, so $\pi_2(e_i)$ equals $\Delta c - e_i$, while if $\Delta c/2 \leq \varepsilon \leq 2\Delta c/3$, the winning price is $(c_1 + 2c_2)/3 + \varepsilon/2$, so that $\pi_2(e_i)$ equals $2\Delta c/3 - \varepsilon/2 + e_i$ (> 0). For $\varepsilon > 2\Delta c/3$, a comparison of equations (11) and (12) reveals that for any e_i, $\pi_2(e_i)$ is positive.

Optimal bidding strategies in the first auction will reflect this equilibrium. Thus, we assume that the bidders are informed in the sense that they know $\pi_2(e_i)$, and make bids in the first auction that are sufficiently high that bidders (weakly) prefer winning to losing in the first auction. On the other hand, when $\varepsilon < 2\Delta c/3$ the first auction symmetric equilibrium cannot result in a bid which results in profits above that associated with these values, since it would always be in one firm's interest to undercut its rival. Hence,

Proposition 4: If $\varepsilon < \Delta c/2$, the first-auction winner wins at a price of c_2, while if $\Delta c/2 \leq \varepsilon \leq 2\Delta c/3$ the first-auction winning bid is $(c_1 + 2c_2)/3 + \varepsilon/2$.

Proposition 4 calculates the first-auction equilibrium when the amount of uncertainty is sufficiently small that each vendor always wins one auction. The first auction equilibrium looks somewhat different when there is more than a small amount of uncertainty.

Proposition 5: If $5\Delta c/3 \geq \varepsilon \geq 2\Delta c/3$, there exists a symmetric equilibrium in the first auction of the form $b_k(e_k)$

$$= \frac{\bar{e}+e_k}{2} + c_1 + \frac{(\bar{e}-e_k)\Delta c}{3\bar{e}} + \frac{2\Delta c^2}{9\bar{e}} + \frac{3(\bar{e}-e_k)^2}{8\bar{e}} \qquad \text{if } e_k \geq \frac{\bar{e}}{3} + \frac{4\Delta c}{9}$$

$$= \frac{(\bar{e}-\underline{e})(3\bar{e}-2\Delta c)}{(\bar{e}-e_k)6\bar{e}} + c_1 + \frac{5\bar{e}}{6} + \frac{10\Delta c}{9} - e_k \qquad \text{if } \frac{\bar{e}}{3} + \frac{4\Delta c}{9} \geq e_k \geq \bar{e} - \frac{2\Delta c}{3}$$

$$= \frac{(\bar{e}-\underline{e})^2(3\bar{e}-2\Delta c)}{6(\bar{e}-e_k)\bar{e}} + \frac{2c_2+c_1}{3} + \frac{2\Delta c^2}{9(\bar{e}-e_k)} + \frac{e_k}{2} + \frac{\bar{e}\underline{e}-\frac{\underline{e}}{2}-\bar{e}e_k+e_k^2}{2(\bar{e}-e_k)} \quad \text{if } e_k \leq \bar{e} - \frac{2\Delta C}{3}$$

Remark: The proof of this proposition involves solving a differential equation. This in turn requires a boundary condition - specifically, the bid associated with $e_k = \check{e}$. I make the assumption that $b_k(\check{e}) - c_1 - \check{e} = \pi_2(\check{e})$. That is, when a bidder has the highest possible costs, its first-auction return equals the expected second period return.[16]

Proof: See Appendix.

The equilibrium in Proposition 5 exists when $5\Delta c/3 \geq \check{e} > 2\Delta c/3$. Together, Propositions 4 and 5 completely characterize the first-auction equilibrium in the sequential auction for $5\Delta c/3 \geq \check{e}$. The equilibria derived in those propositions are relevant in the range for which the asymmetric equilibrium exists in the simultaneous auction. Note that for $5\Delta c/3 \leq \check{e}$, a different symmetric equilibrium exists in the sequential auction.

3. Comparison of Prices and Welfare Under Alternative Equilibria

The previous section derived equilibrium under two alternative auction regimes; one in which auctions are held simultaneously, and one in which auctions are held sequentially. These two equilibrium will differ

---

[16] This assumption appears to be common in the auction literature (see McAfee and MacMillan (1987) or Riley and Samuelson (1981)). The logic is readily apparent when the distribution of e has an atom at $\check{e}$. In that case, a symmetric equilibrium must be characterized by $b(\check{e}) - c_1 - \check{e} = \pi_2(\check{e})$, if $b(e)$ is monotonic, since each bidder knows the only way it can win is if the other bidder draws $\check{e}$ as well. When both bidders have $\check{e}$ as their cost parameter, a bid by j above $c_1 + \check{e} + \pi_2(\check{e})$ will always induce i to shade. Conversely, if j bids $c_1 + \check{e} + \pi_2(\check{e})$, i cannot win if it bids above that amount. The logic is not altered by allowing the atom to become arbitrarily small.

both in the prices charged and in the resulting production cost. The price comparison would naturally be of interest to a buyer with multiple projects. A buyer who knew that one of these two equilibrium would emerge, depending on which regime it chose, would of course select the one which resulted in lower prices. As shown is section 3.A, if the buyer knows the asymmetric equilibrium will emerge, it will prefer simultaneous auctions, as the expected bids are lower in that regime than in the sequential one.

The other question of interest is which auction regime is likely to result in lower production costs. Perhaps surprisingly, the sequential auction will yield lower production costs than the simultaneous auction. The intuition can be seen most readily when $4\Delta c/9 \leq \tilde{e} < 2\Delta c/3$. When the amount of uncertainty falls in this range, it is always efficient to have each vendor win one bid. As detailed in Propositions 2 and 3, the equilibrium to the sequential auction implies that each vendor will win one bid each whenever $\tilde{e} < 2\Delta c/3$. Conversely, as long as $\tilde{e} \geq 4\Delta c/9$, the probability is non-zero that one vendor will win both bids in the simultaneous auction. Hence, for $\tilde{e}$ in this range, efficient production always occurs in the sequential auction, but not necessarily in the simultaneous auction. Within the framework presented in section 2, this implies that welfare is higher under the sequential auction than the simultaneous auction, although a buyer would choose the simultaneous auction. In that framework, buyers have inelastic demand, so that price does not affect the number of projects chosen. More generally, if the buyer had a downward-sloping demand for projects (e.g., a reservation value), there may be a welfare trade-off (productive vs. allocative efficiency) in choosing between the auction regimes.

One unusual feature of the equilibrium in the simultaneous auction equilibrium is that similarly-situated individuals behave asymmetrically. As the equilibrium is not unique (there are at least two asymmetric equilibria - i.e., one with j bidding a common amount, and one with i bidding a common amount), it is possible that a symmetric equilibrium exists as well. In fact, a recent paper by Lang and Rosenthal (1991) develop a mixed-strategy equilibrium in a similar context.

The Lang and Rosenthal model differs from that of this paper in that there is no uncertainty regarding cost, but there is a cost of making a bid. In their model, a mixed strategy symmetric equilibrium emerges in which each bidder randomizes its lower bid, and makes a second bid if its lower bid is above some value. For the range of lower bids where a second bid is made, the second bid is a decreasing function of the first bid. This helps solve the coordination problem since the bidder with the lower first bid cannot win the second bid. On the other hand, there is the potential that neither bidder makes a second bid, and in that case, there is a 50% probability that one project does not get produced.

The costliness of bidding is essential to their model; without some cost to make a bid the equilibrium will not be as described. In fact, there may be no equilibrium if bidding is costless. Conversely, all of the equilibria in this paper are contingent on costless bidding. Hence, the results of Lang and Rosenthal cannot readily be compared to those in this paper.

A. Prices Under Alternative Auctions Regimes

As discussed above, prices will be higher in a sequential equilibrium than in the asymmetric simultaneous equilibrium. The intuition for this result can be seen most clearly when $4\Delta c/9 \leq \varepsilon \leq 2\Delta c/3$. Let player 2's realization of the uncertainty parameter e_i, be lower than player 1's (i.e., $e_2 < e_1$). When $4\Delta c/9 \leq \varepsilon \leq 2\Delta c/3$, there is no real uncertainty in the sequential auction, since bidder 1 always wins the second auction. When $\varepsilon < 2\Delta c/3$, bidder 1 possesses a cost advantage, in that it knows it will be the lower-cost bidder (given that the bidder 2 already won one auction). As a result, bidder 1's winning bid in the second auction is equal to the minimum potential value of player 2's bid for a second project, as shown in Propositions 2 and 4.

Conversely, in the simultaneous auction when ε is in this range, neither bidder knows how many bids it will win. Consequently, the bid functions reflects the possibility that a higher bid may result in a lower probability of winning. When $\Delta c/2 \leq \varepsilon \leq 2\Delta c/3$, the sum of the winning bids in the sequential auction is $(4c_2 + 2c_1)/3 + \varepsilon$, while the maximum possible value in the simultaneous auction is $(5c_1 + 3c_2)/4 + (29/16)\varepsilon$, which is less than $(4c_2 + 2c_1)/3 + \varepsilon$ for $\varepsilon < 28/37\Delta c$.[17] Hence the sum of the bids in the simultaneous auction is less than in the sequential auction for $\varepsilon < 2\Delta c/3$.

For values of ε greater than $2\Delta c/3$, the expression for the sum of the winning bids in the sequential

---

[17] When $4\Delta c/9 < \varepsilon < \Delta c/2$, the same conclusion holds.

auction becomes more complicated. Nonetheless, the conclusion holds that prices are higher in the sequential equilibrium. The expressions in Table 1 represent the sum of the winning bids in the sequential equilibrium minus the sum in the asymmetric simultaneous equilibrium, for alternative values of e_i and e_j. In each case, the expression can be shown to be positive for all relevant value of $\check{e}$ (i.e., for $2\Delta c/3 \leq \check{e} \leq 4\Delta c/3$).[18]

This analysis implies that <u>if</u> the buyer knew that the asymmetric equilibrium would emerge, it would choose to use simultaneous auctions instead of sequential ones. However, as noted, the asymmetric equilibrium is not unique as there are at least two asymmetric equilibria and perhaps a symmetric one as well. Thus, the conclusion that buyers choose simultaneous auctions because they know lower prices will emerge rests on the assumption that a specific equilibrium will emerge.

One justification for this assumption is the empirical observation of the bids portrayed in figure 1, along with evidence that increasing costs do appear relevant to the industries in question. Although it is not clear how such an equilibrium emerged, both bidders and the buyer will have their expectations confirmed if they believe the equilibrium will persist.

A perhaps more satisfying justification could be based on introducing a dynamic element to the model. For example, suppose that there is a single incumbent seller facing an entrant. If possible, the incumbent will attempt to commit to a bid function featuring identical bids on the two projects.[19] If such a commitment is credable, the asymmetric equilibrium will emerge after entry.

Finally, recall that the asymmetric equilibrium only exists if the amount of uncertainty is small relative to the slope of costs. Hence, one prediction of the model is that even when costs are increasing, sequential auctions will tend to be used when costs are subject to considerable uncertainty. One would expect more uncertainty for projects which are complex, such as those procured by the military, rather than the type procured by local governments or building contractors.

---

[18] For example, when $\check{e} < e_i < \Delta c/2 - \check{e}/8$ and $\check{e} < e_j < \check{e}$, the difference can be written $4\Delta c/9 + \check{e}/3 + 3\,e_{max}/4 - e_{min} - e_j/2$. Since $e_{max} \geq e_{min}$, this expression is greater than $4\Delta c/9 + \check{e}/3 - e_{min}/4 - e_j/2$, which is positive since both e_{min} and e_j are less than $\check{e}$ $(= 4\Delta c/9 + \check{e}/3)$.

[19] In the equilibrium of Proposition 1, bidder j's profits exceeds those of bidder i.

B. Production Costs Under Alternative Equilibria

The Introduction discussed how the existence of increasing costs led to a type of coordination problem. While total production costs may be minimized by one bidder winning one-half the projects, each bidder cannot know how many projects he will win. If a symmetric, pure strategy equilibrium emerges, where bids are increasing functions of costs, a small difference in costs will lead to one bidder winning both bids with a probability of one-half.[20]

In section 2, I derived two alternative equilibria which might alleviate the coordination problem. One way of seeing the impact of alternative equilibria is to compare the likelihood that production cost is not minimized. Suppose that $e_1 > e_2$, so that bidder 1 has a cost schedule which lies above that of bidder 2. Social cost is minimized by vender 2 winning both auctions if and only if $\Delta c < e_1 - e_2$. When $\overline{e} < \Delta c$, this condition cannot be satisfied, and it is always efficient to have each vendor produce one project.

The probability that one bidder wins both projects under the sequential auction is

$$\frac{1}{\overline{e}} \int_{\frac{\overline{e}}{3}+\frac{4\Delta c}{9}}^{\overline{e}} \frac{1}{e_1} \int_0^{\frac{3e_1}{2}-\frac{\overline{e}}{2}-\frac{2\Delta c}{3}} de_2 \, de_1.$$

In the asymmetric equilibrium, let $x = e_j - e_i$. Using equation 7A - 7D, one player wins both auctions when $\Delta c/2 + \overline{e}/8 < x < \overline{e}/8 - \Delta c/2$, so that the probability of inefficient production is

$$\int_{\frac{\Delta c}{2}+\frac{\overline{e}}{8}}^{\min(\overline{e},\Delta c)} \left(\frac{1}{\overline{e}}-\frac{x}{\overline{e}^2}\right) dx + \int_{-\max(\overline{e},\Delta c)}^{\frac{\overline{e}}{8}-\frac{\Delta c}{2}} \left(\frac{1}{\overline{e}}+\frac{x}{\overline{e}^2}\right) dx.$$

---

[20] As we have not demonstrated the existence of a symmetric equilibrium, the symmetric case can be view as a benchmark with which to compare the alternative equilibrium.

Table 2 compares the probability that one bidder wins both auctions under these two equilibria for alternative values of ε ($< \Delta c$). Note that the probability of inefficient production is always lower for the sequential equilibrium, but the asymmetric equilibrium still results in probability well below the 50% probability associated with the symmetric equilibrium.

This suggests the sequential equilibrium results in lower production costs than the asymmetric equilibrium, which in turn is lower than the symmetric equilibrium. These conclusion remain when expected costs are explicitly calculated. Table 3 calculates the difference in expected costs between those resulting from the equilibria to the auction in question and those that minimize production costs. For example, if $\varepsilon = .85$ and $\Delta c = 1$, the expected excess costs (above those that minimize production costs) associated with the asymmetric equilibrium are .078, while the excess costs associated with the sequential equilibrium are .004. Figures 5 and 6 show the excess production costs for each auction for alternative values of ε.

4. Conclusion

This paper developed a model of bidding for multiple projects under increasing costs. Such a model appears applicable to certain products regularly purchased through auctions by government agencies. When bidders have increasing costs, it will generally be desirable to allocate projects evenly across bidders. The results of this paper suggest that any auction mechanism may fail to optimally allocate projects. Further, the analysis suggests that the auction regime rationally chosen by buyers may result in higher expected production costs than alternative regimes available to them.

These results, as well as other recent work, suggest that noncooperative behavior can lead to bids that may appear to result from collusion. Further, this paper modeled the simplest type of interdependency across projects. The noncooperative equilibrium may consist of more complicated bids when cost interdependencies are related to optimal routing of delivery trucks or lumpiness in production facilities. Absent a clear notion of what the non cooperative equilibrium looks like, antitrust enforcement based on finding "suspicious" bidding patterns seems ill-advised.

APPENDIX

Proof of Lemma 1: To derive i's optimal bid functions, I first calculate the probabilities in equation 1. Since player j bids the same amount on both projects, and those bids are linear functions of e_j (see Lemma 2), $b^j = b^j_1 = b^j_2$ will be uniform as well. Without loss of generality let $b^i_1 \leq b^i_2$. Then

$P(W,L) = \text{Prob } (b^i_1 < b^j < b^i_2) =$

$$\int_{b^i_1}^{\min(b^j(\bar{e}),b^i_2)} f(b^j)db^j = (\min(b^i_2,b^j(\bar{e})) - b^i_1)/(b^j(\bar{e}) - b^j(0)).$$

$P(W,W) = \text{Prob } (b^i_2 < b^j) =$

$$\int_{b^i_2}^{\max(b^j(\bar{e}), b^i_2)} f(b^j)db^j = (\max (b^j(\bar{e}),b^i_2) - b^i_2)/(b^j(\bar{e}) - b^j(0)).$$

and $P(L,W) = 0$.

Using these probabilities bidder i's objective function is

(A.1) $\pi = 1/(b^j(\bar{e}) - b^j(0)) [(b^i_1 - c_1 - e_i) (bi2 - b^i_1) + (b^i_1 + b^i_2 - c_1 - c_2 - 2e_i) (bj(\bar{e}) - bi2)] + \lambda_1 (b^i_1 - b^j(0)) + \lambda_2 (b^j(\bar{e}) - b^i_2)$

For values of e_i which satisfy the two constraints, the first-order conditions are

$$(A.2) \quad \partial\pi/\partial b^i_1 = \frac{[(b^i_1 - c_1 - e_i)(-1) + (b^i_2 - b^i_1) + (b^j(\bar{e}) - b^i_2)]}{(b^j(\bar{e}) - b^j(0))} = 0$$

$$(A.3) \quad \partial\pi/\partial b^i_2 = \frac{(b^i_1 - c_1 - e_i) - (b^i_2 + b^i_1 - c_1 - c_2 - 2e_i) + (b^j(\bar{e}) - b^i_2)}{(b^j(\bar{e}) - b^j(0))} = 0$$

so that player i chooses b^i_1 and b^i_2 to satisfy

(A.4) $b^i_1 = (c_1 + e_i + b^j(\bar{e}))/2$

(A.5) $b^i_2 = (c_2 + e_i + b^j(\bar{e}))/2.$

Note that if $e_i < 2b^j(0) - c_1 - b^j(\bar{e})$, A.2 implies $b_1^i < b^j$ which violates the first constraint. Hence i's optimal bids are

(2) $\quad b_1^i = (c_1 + e_i + b^j(\bar{e}))/2 \quad$ if $e_i \geq 2b^j(0) - c_1 - b^j(\bar{e}) \equiv \hat{e}$

$\qquad\quad = b^j(0) \qquad\qquad$ if $e_i \leq \hat{e}$

(3) $\quad b_2^i = (c_2 + e_i + b^j(\bar{e}))/2.\blacksquare$

Proof of Lemma 2: Bidder j's objective function is

(A.6) $\pi = (b_1^j - c_1 - e^j) P(W,L) + (b_2^j - c_1 - e^j) P(L,W) + (b_1^j + b_2^j - c_1 - c_2 - 2 e^j) P(W,W)$

Since i's bids are both increasing in e_i, the probability of j winning a bid is not independent of the outcome in the other auction. In fact since the difference between i's higher and lower bid will be $\Delta c/2$ over some range, the probability in (A.6) will depend on whether j's bids are more or less than $\Delta c/2$ apart. In what follows I assume that j's bids are less than $\Delta c/2$ apart. It can be shown that j's profit from bids less than $\Delta c/2$ apart (i.e., equations 5 and 6) are higher than the profit from optimal bids when those bids are constrained to be more than $\Delta c/2$ apart.

To derive j's optimal reactions, it is necessary to develop expressions for the probabilities in (A.6). Since bidder j does not know which project has the lower bidder i bid, the likelihood that j is bidding against i's lower bid is the same on the two projects. Hence the probability that j wins both bids is

$P(W,W) = 1/2 \, P(W,W|b_1^i < b_2^i) + 1/2 \, P(W,W|b_1^i > b_2^i) = 1/2 \, P[(b_1^j < b_1^i), (b_2^j < b_2^i)|b_1^i < b_2^i] + 1/2 \, P[(b_1^j < b_1^i), (b_2^j < b_2^i)|b_1^i > b_2^i].$

Evaluating the two conditional probabilities separately, first suppose that $b_1^i < b_2^i$

i) If $b_1^i < b_2^i$ then since $b_2^i < b_1^i + \Delta c/2$, j's winning the first bid implies it wins the second bid so that $P(W,W) = P[(b_1^j < b_1^i)] \equiv P[(b_1^j < b_L^i)].$

If $b_1^i(0) > b_1^i(\bar{e})$ (as shown in Proposition 1, this requires $\bar{e} < 4\Delta c/3$), then j can only win when $e_i > \hat{e}$, and this probability becomes

Since b_L^i is a linear function of e_i for $e_i > \hat{e}$ with $\partial b_L^i/\partial e_i = 1/2$, this equals $2(b_L^i(\bar{e}) - b_1^j)/\bar{e}.$

20

$$P(W,W) = P(b_1^j < b_1^i) = \frac{\bar{e} - \hat{e}}{\bar{e}} \int_{b_1^j}^{b_L^i(\bar{e})} f(b_L^i) db_L^i = \frac{b_L^i(\bar{e}) - b_1^j}{\bar{e}} \frac{\bar{e} - \hat{e}}{b_L^i(\bar{e}) - b_L^i(\hat{e})}$$

ii) If $b_1^i > b_2^i$ and $b_1^j < b_2^j + \Delta c/2$

$P(W,W) = P(b_2^j < b_L^i)$. If $b_2^j(0) > b_2^i(\hat{e})$, this probability is

$$P(b_2^j < b_L^i) = \frac{\bar{e} - \hat{e}}{\bar{e}} \int_{b_2^j}^{b_L^i(\bar{e})} f(b_L^i) db_L^i = \frac{b_L^i(\bar{e}) - b_2^j}{\bar{e}} \frac{\bar{e} - \hat{e}}{b_L^i(\bar{e}) - b_L^i(\hat{e})} = \frac{2(b_L^i(\bar{e}) - b_2^j)}{\bar{e}}$$

Since the two cases are equally likely, $P(W,W) =$

$$= \frac{2b_L^i(\bar{e}) - b_1^j - b_2^j}{\bar{e}}.$$

In calculating $P(W,L)$, the sign of $b_1^i - b_2^i$ is again relevant. $P(W,L) = P[b_1^j < b_1^i$ and $b_2^i < b_2^j]$.

i) If $b_1^i > b_2^i$ and $b_2^j < b_1^j + \Delta c/2$, then recalling the

relationship between b_1^i and b_2^i, j will win the first bid but lose the second if $b_1^j < b_H^i < b_2^j + \Delta c/2$ for $e_i > \hat{e}$. Similarly, for $e_i < \hat{e}$ (assuming $b_2^j(0) < b_2^i(\hat{e})$), j will win the first bid and lose the second if $b_1^j < b_H^i$, so that

$$P(W,L) = \frac{\bar{e} - \hat{e}}{\bar{e}} \int_{b_1^j}^{b_2^j + \frac{\Delta c}{2}} f(b_H^i) db_H^i + \frac{\hat{e}}{\bar{e}} \int_{b_1^j}^{b_H^i(\hat{e})} f(b_H^i) db_H^i =$$

$$\frac{\bar{e} - \hat{e}}{b_H^i(\bar{e}) - b_H^i(\hat{e})} \frac{b_2^j + \frac{\Delta c}{2} - b_1^j}{\bar{e}} + \frac{\hat{e}}{b_H^i(\hat{e}) - b_H^i(0)} \frac{b_H^i(\hat{e}) - b_1^j}{\bar{e}} = \frac{2(b_2^j + \frac{\Delta c}{2} - 2b_1^j + b_H^i(\hat{e}))}{\bar{e}}$$

ii) if $b_1^i < b_2^i$, and $b_1^i < b_2^j + \Delta c/2$, $P(W,L) = 0$.

Since it is equally likely that $b_1^i < b_2^i$ or $b_1^i > b_2^i$, $P(W,L)$ equals

$$\frac{(b_2^j + \frac{\Delta c}{2} - 2b_1^j + b_H^i(\bar{e})}{\bar{e}}$$

Symmetrically, $P(L,W)$ equals

$$\frac{(b_1^j + \frac{\Delta c}{2} - 2b_2^j + b_H^i(\bar{e}))}{\bar{e}}$$

Given these probabilities, differentiating equation A.6 with respect to b_1^j and b_2^j yields the following first-order conditions:

A.7) $(b_1^j - c_1 - e_j)(-2) + (b_2^j + \Delta c/2 - 2b_1^j + b_H^i(\bar{c})) + (b_2^j - c_1 - e_j)$

$- (b_1^j + b_2^j - c_1 - c_2 - 2e_j) + (2b_L^i(\bar{e}) - b_1^j - b_2^j) = 0$

A.8) $(b_1^j - c_1 - e_j) + (b_1^j + \Delta c/2 - 2b_2^j + b_H^i(\bar{c})) - 2(b_2^j - c_1 - e_j)$

$- (b_1^j + b_2^j - c_1 - c_2 - 2e_j) + (2b_L^i(\bar{e}) - b_1^j - b_2^j) = 0$

solving for b_1^j and b_2^j yields

(5) $b_1^j = (c_1 + c_2)/4 + e_j/2 + (b_H^i(\bar{c}) + 2b_L^i(\bar{e}))/6$

(6) $b_2^j = (c_1 + c_2)/4 + e_j/2 + (b_H^i(\bar{c}) + 2b_L^i(\bar{e}))/6$.

Thus, if b_1^i and b_2^i are constrained to be at most $\Delta c/2$ apart, j's optimal strategy is to be bid the same amount on both projects. When the bids are constrained to be at least $\Delta c/2$ apart, the optimal bids turn out to be exactly $\Delta c/2$ apart. Since this same profit is available when j's bids are constrained to be at most $\Delta c/2$ apart, the profit resulting from identical bids (as in 5 and 6) is greater than that associated with bids $\Delta c/2$ apart.∎

Proof of Proposition 3: Given $\bar{e} > \Delta c/2$, the first-auction winner, j solves

22

Max $\pi_j = (b_j - c_2 - e_j) \, \text{Prob}(b_j < b_i)$

For $e_j < \check{e}$, the probability that $b_j < b_i$ is

$$Prob \ (b_j < b_i) = \frac{\check{e} - e_j}{\bar{e} - e_j} \int_{\min(b_i(\check{e}), b_j)}^{b_i(\check{e})} f_1(b_i) db_i \ + \ \frac{\bar{e} - \check{e}}{\bar{e} - e_j} \int_{\max(b_j, b_i(\check{e}))}^{b_i(\bar{e})} f_2(b_i) db_i$$

Where f_1 is the density of $b_i(e_i)$ for $e_i < \check{e}$ and f_2 is the density of $b_i(e_i)$ for $e_i > \check{e}$. If i bids as in equation 11 so that $b_j > b_i(\check{e})$,

$$Prob \ (b_j < b_i) = \frac{\check{e} - e_j}{\bar{e} - e_j} \cdot 0 \ + \ \frac{\bar{e} - \check{e}}{\bar{e} - e_j} \int_{b_j}^{b_i(\bar{e})} f_2(b_i) db_i.$$

Since b_i is distributed uniformly for $e_i > \check{e}$, this can be written

$$\frac{\bar{e} - \check{e}}{\bar{e} - e_j} \frac{b_i(\bar{e}) - b_j}{b_i(\bar{e}) - b_i(\check{e})} = \frac{b_i(\bar{e}) - b_j}{\bar{e} - e_j} \cdot \eta \quad for \ e_j < \check{e}$$

$$where \ \eta = \frac{\bar{e} - \check{e}}{b_i(\bar{e}) - b_i(\check{e})}$$

Hence, j's maximization becomes

$$\max_{b_j} \ \Pi_j = (b_j - c_2 - e_j)(b_i(\bar{e}) - b_j) \cdot \frac{\eta}{\bar{e} - e_j}$$

and the first-order condition for a maximum is

A.9) $b_j = (c_2 + e_j + b_i(\check{e}))/2 \qquad$ for $e_j < \check{e}$.

By construction, for $e_j > \check{e}$ there are no profitable bids for bidder j. Hence, a computationally-simple assumption is that j plays the weakly dominant strategy of bidding as in equation A.9 for all e_j.

The first-auction loser, bidder i maximizes

Max $\pi_i = (b_i - c_1 - e_i) \, \text{Prob}(b_i < b_j)$

If $e_i \geq \check{e}$

23

$$Prob \ (b_i < b_j) = \int_{b_i}^{b_j(e_i)} f(b_j) db_j$$

Given j's strategy, b_j is a linear function of e_j so this probability becomes

$$= \frac{b_j(e_i) - b_i}{b_j(e_i) - b_j(0)}.$$

Hence, i's maximization can be rewritten

Max $\pi_i = (b_i - c_1 - e_i)[(b_j(\breve{e}) - b_i)]/(b_j(e_i) - b_j(0)) + \lambda(b_i - b_j(0))$

and the first-order conditions for a maximum are

A.10) $b_i = (c_1 + e_i + b_j(e_i))/2 + \lambda$

and $b_i > b_j(0)$.

Solving A.9) and A.10) simultaneously yields

A.9') $b_j = (c_1 + 2c_2)/3 + (e_j + \breve{e})/2$

A.10') $b_i = (2c_1 + c_2)/3 + (3e_i + \breve{e})/4$ for $e_i > \breve{e}$

Hence, the second-auction equilibrium is

11) $b_i = \quad (2c_1 + c_2)/3 + (3e_i + \breve{e})/4$ for $e_i \geq \breve{e}$

$\quad\quad\quad (c_1 + 2c_2)/3 + \breve{e}/2 \quad\quad$ for $e_i \leq \breve{e}$

12) $b_j = \quad (c_1 + 2c_2)/3 + (e_j + \breve{e})/2$

where $\breve{e} = \breve{e}/3 + 4\Delta c/9$, $\grave{e} = \breve{e} - 2\Delta c/3$ ∎

Proof of Proposition 5

Given the second-auction equilibrium, player k (=i,j) maximizes

$\pi_1^k = (b_k - c_1 - e_k - \pi_2^k) \, Prob(b_k < b_{not \, k})$

subject to $(b_k - c_1 - e_k) > \pi_2^k$

where $\pi_2^k \ (> 0)$ is the difference in second-auction profits between losing and winning the first auction. The probability term in the objective function can be rewritten

24

$\text{Prob}(b_k < b_{\text{not } k}) = 1 - F(B^{-1}(b_k)),$

where B is k's bidding function. If a symmetric equilibrium is to hold in the first auction, $b_k = B(e_k)$, so that the objective function can be rewritten

A.11) $\pi_1^k = (b_k - c_1 - e_k - \pi_2^k)(1 - F(e_k)).$

Taking the derivative with respect to e_k yields the bidding function,

A.12) $d\pi/de_k = (F(e_k) - 1)(1 + \partial\pi_2^k/\partial e_k)$

To solve this first-order differential equation, note when $\check{e} \le 5\Delta c/3$, $\check{e} \le \check{e}$, so that equations (11) and (12) imply that $\pi_2^k(e_k) =$

$\Delta c/3[2 - (\check{e} - e_k)/(\check{e} - e_k)] + (\bar{e} - e_k - \check{e})/2 \quad$ for $e_k < \check{e}$

$2\Delta c/3 + \bar{e}/2 - e_k \quad\quad\quad\quad$ for $\check{e} < e_k < \check{e}$

$[\Delta c/3 - (\bar{e} - e_k)/4][3(\bar{e} - e_k)/2 + 2\,\Delta c/3]/\bar{e} \quad$ for $e_k > \check{e}.$

a) For $e_k \ge \check{e}$, the solution to the differential equation in A.12) equals

$$\int_e^{\bar{e}} \frac{d\Pi}{de}\ dx = \int_e^{\bar{e}} (F(x)-1)(1 - \frac{2\Delta C}{3\bar{e}})\ dx$$

$$\Rightarrow A.13)\quad \Pi(\bar{e}) - \Pi(e) = \int_e^{\bar{e}} (F(x)-1)\ (1 - \frac{2\Delta C}{3\bar{e}})dx.$$

The assumption that $\pi(\bar{e}) \equiv [b_k(\bar{e}) - c_1 - \bar{e} - \pi_2^k(\bar{e})] = 0$ means that equation A.13) can be rewritten

$$A.14)\quad \Pi(e) = \int_e^{\bar{e}} (1 - F(x))\ dx(1 - \frac{2\Delta C}{3\bar{e}}).$$

and using equation A.11,

Since $1 - F(x) = (\bar{e} - x)/\bar{e}$, the integral on the right-hand side equals

25

$$A.15) \quad b_k(e) = \frac{\int_e^{\bar{e}} (1 - F(x)) dx (1 - \frac{2\Delta c}{3\bar{e}})}{(1 - F(e))} + \pi_2^k(e) + c_1 + e_k.$$

$$\text{using the fact that } \int_{e_k}^{\bar{e}} (1 - F(x)) dx = \frac{\int_e^{\bar{e}} (\bar{e} - x) dx}{\bar{e}} = \frac{(\bar{e} - e_k)^2}{2\bar{e}}$$

Hence, using the definitions of F(x) and π_2^k,

$$A.16) \quad b_k = c_1 + e_k + \frac{\bar{e} - e_k}{2}(1 - \frac{2\Delta c}{3\bar{e}}) + (\frac{\Delta c}{3} + \frac{\bar{e} - e_k}{4})(\frac{\frac{3(\bar{e} - e_k)}{2} + \frac{2\Delta C}{3}}{\bar{e}})$$

$$= c_1 + \frac{\bar{e} + e_k}{2} + \frac{(\bar{e} - e_k)\Delta c}{3\bar{e}} + \frac{2\Delta c^2}{9\bar{e}} + \frac{3(\bar{e} - e_k)^2}{8\bar{e}}.$$

b) When $\check{e} \leq e \leq \check{e}$, $\partial \pi_2^k / \partial e_k = 1$, so that the right-hand side of equation A.12) equal zero. That is, the sum of the production cost and the opportunity cost of winning (π_2^k) is the same for all e in this range. To calculate the equilibrium bids, we note that since the total cost the same for all e, it must be the case that the expected profit is the same for all e in that range. In particular,

$$\frac{\bar{e} - e_k}{\bar{e}}[b_k(e_k) - e_k - c_1 - \pi_2^k] = \frac{\bar{e} - \check{e}}{\bar{e}}[b_k(\check{e}) - \check{e} - c_1 - \pi_2^k(\check{e})]$$

$$<=> \quad b_k = \frac{\check{e} - e_k}{\bar{e} - e_k}[e_k + c_1 + \pi_2^k(\check{e})] + \frac{\bar{e} - \check{e}}{\bar{e} - e_k} b_k(\check{e})$$

since $e_k + \pi_2(e_k) = \check{e} + \pi_2^k(\check{e})$. From equation A.16) we know

Hence

26

$$b_k(\check{e}) = c_1 + \check{e} + \pi_2^k(\check{e}) + \frac{\bar{e} - \check{e}}{2} \frac{3\bar{e} - 2\Delta c}{6\bar{e}}$$

$$b_k(e_k) = \frac{(\bar{e} - \check{e})^2}{\bar{e} - e_k} \frac{3\bar{e} - 2\Delta c}{6\bar{e}} + \check{e} + c_1 + \pi_2^k(\check{e})$$

A.17)
$$= \frac{(\bar{e} - \check{e})^2(3\bar{e} - 2\Delta c)}{6\bar{e}(\bar{e} - e_k)} + \frac{2c_2 + c_1}{3} + \frac{\bar{e}}{2} - e_k + \frac{\bar{e}}{3} + \frac{4\Delta c}{9}$$

Such a bid represents an equilibrium since no alternative bid yields higher profits (although for most

e in this range, small increases or decreases from this strategy yield equal profits).

c) For $e_k < \check{e}$, the solution to A.12) equals

$$\pi(e) = \pi(\check{e}) + \frac{\int_{\check{e}}^{\bar{e}}(1 - F(x))dx}{2} = \pi(\check{e}) + \frac{1}{2\bar{e}}[\bar{e}\check{e} - \frac{\check{e}^2}{2} - \bar{e}e + \frac{e^2}{2}]$$

$$\Rightarrow b_k(e_k) = \pi(\check{e})\frac{\bar{e}}{\bar{e} - e} + c_1 + e_k + \pi_2^k(e_k) + \frac{\bar{e}\check{e} - \frac{\check{e}^2}{2} - \bar{e}e + \frac{e^2}{2}}{2(\bar{e} - e}$$

Using A.17 and the definition of $\pi_2(e_k)$

$$b_k(e_k) = \frac{(\bar{e} - \check{e})^2(3\bar{e} - 2\Delta c)}{6(\bar{e} - e_k)\bar{e}} + \frac{2c_2 + c_1}{3} + \frac{2\Delta c^2}{9(\bar{e} - e_k)} + \frac{e_k}{2} + \frac{\bar{e}\check{e} - \frac{\check{e}^2}{2} - \bar{e}e_k + \frac{e_k^2}{2}}{2(\bar{e} - e_k)} \blacksquare$$

BIBLIOGRAPHY:

Anton, James J. and Dennis A. Yao "Split Awards, Procurement, and Innovation" <u>Rand Journal of Economics</u> 20, pp. 538-552 (1989).

Bernheim, B. Douglas and Michael D. Whinston "Menu Auctions, Resource Allocation, and Economic Influence" <u>Quarterly Journal of Economics</u> 101, pp. 1-31 (1986).

Kendricks, Kenneth and Robert Porter "Collusion in Auctions" <u>Annales D'Economie et de Statistique</u> 15-16, pp. 217-230 (1989).

Lang, Kevin and Robert W. Rosenthal "The Contractors' Game" <u>Rand Journal of Economics</u> 22, pp. 329-338 (1991).

McAfee, R. Preston and John McMillan "Auctions" <u>Journal of Economic Literature</u> 25, pp. 699-738 (1981)

Riley, John G. and William F. Samuelson "Optimal Auctions" <u>American Economic Review</u> 71, pp.381-392 (1981).

Rothrock, Thomas P., James T. McClave and Janet Ailstock "A Computerized Economic and Statistical Review of the Florida School Board Market" <u>Southeast Antitrust Review</u> pp. 13-54 (Autumn, 1978)

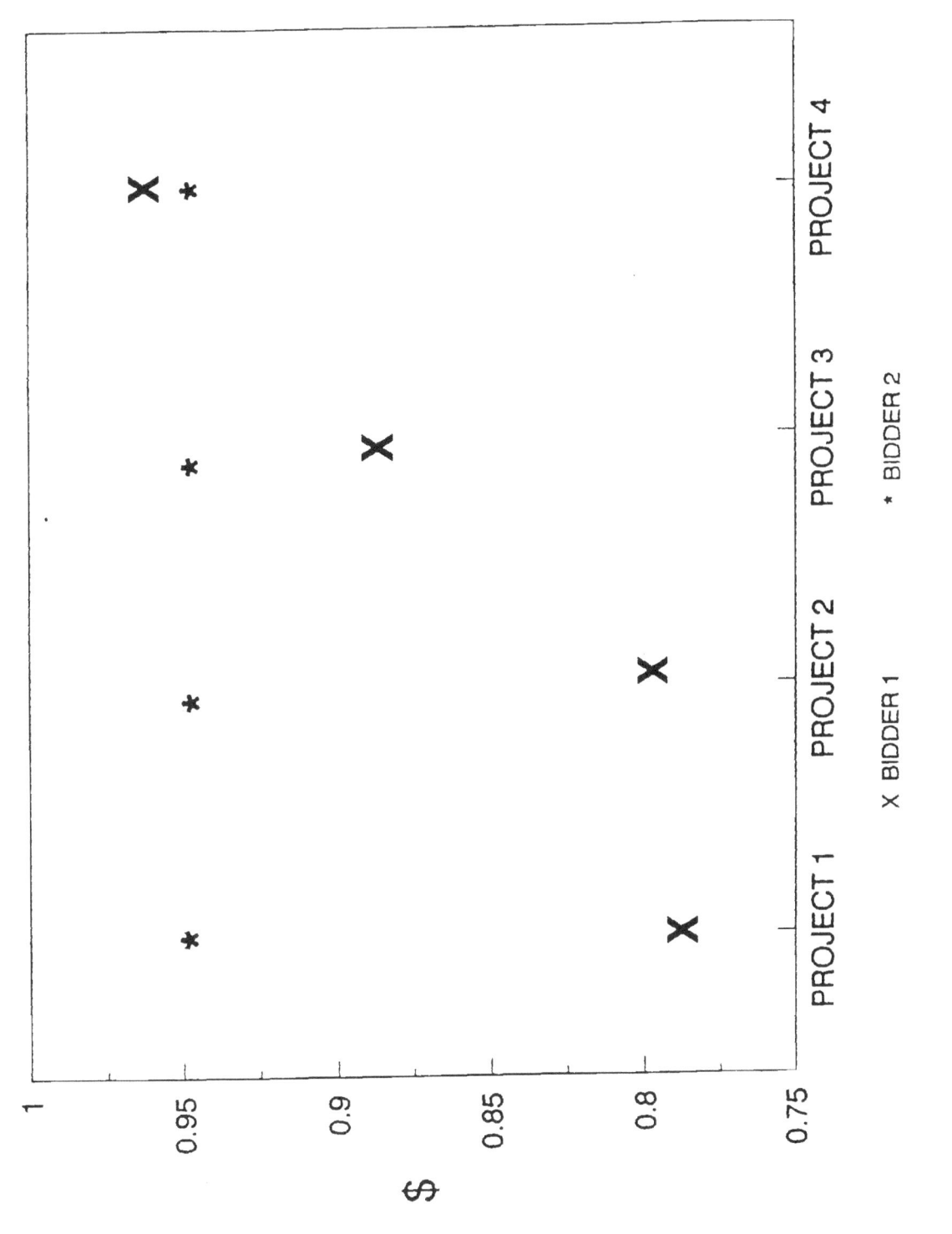

BIDS IN SIMULTANEOUS AUCTIONS

X BIDDER 1   * BIDDER 2

FIGURE 1

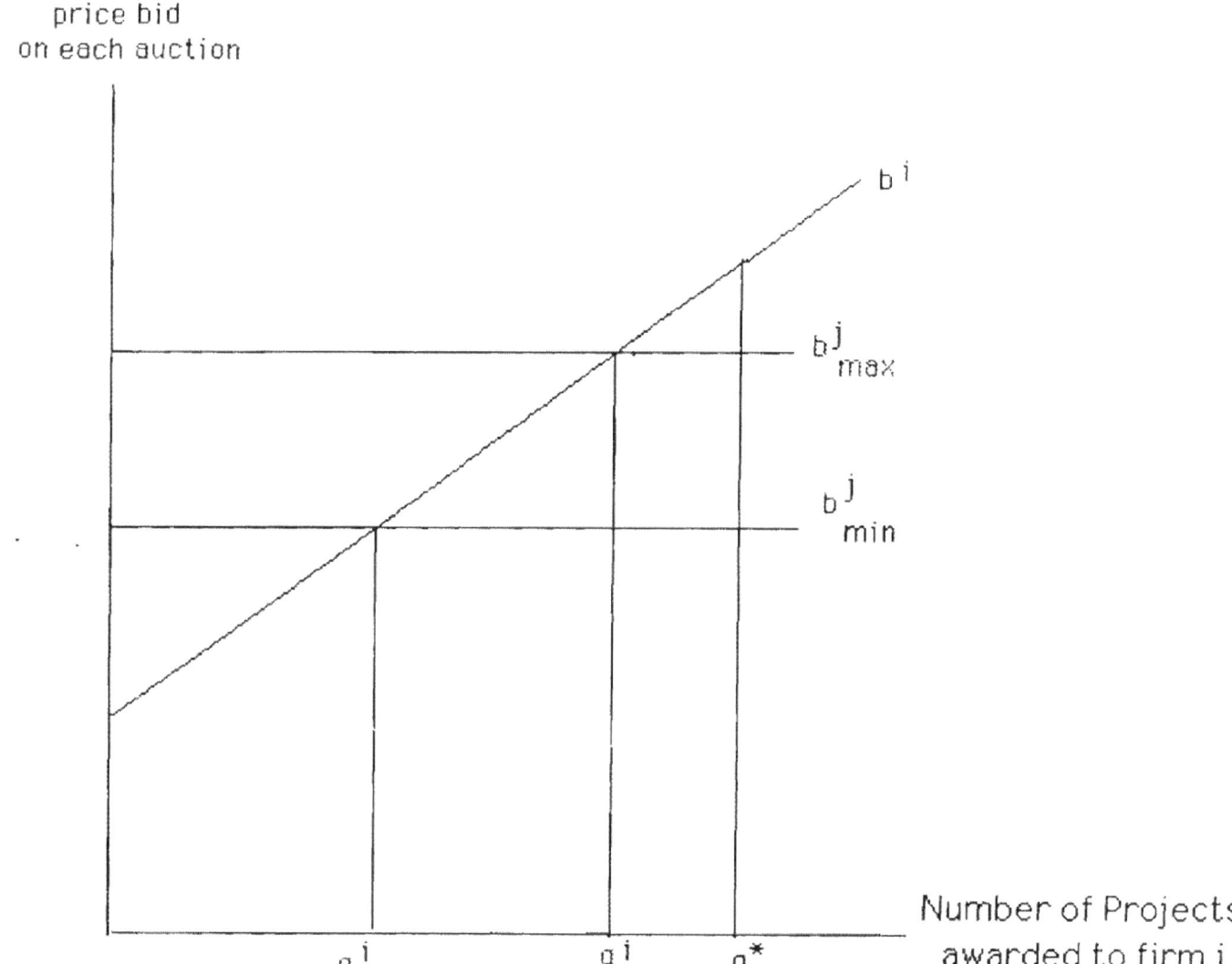

price bid
on each auction

b^i

b^j_{max}

b^j_{min}

q^i_{min}

q^i_{max}

q^*

Number of Projects
awarded to firm i

FIGURE 2

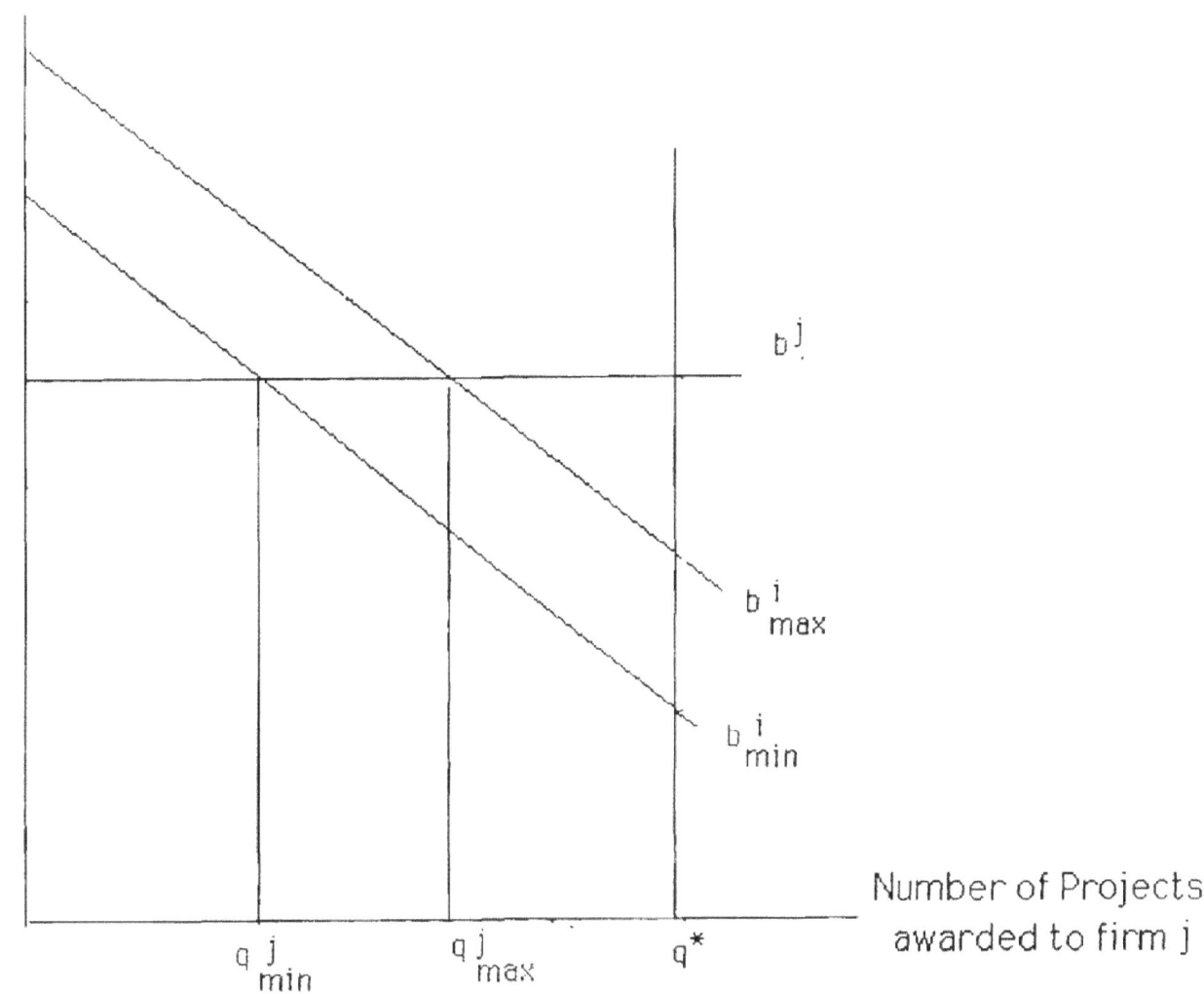

price bid
on each auction

b^j

b^i_{max}

b^i_{min}

Number of Projects
awarded to firm j

q^j_{min} q^j_{max} q^*

FIGURE 3

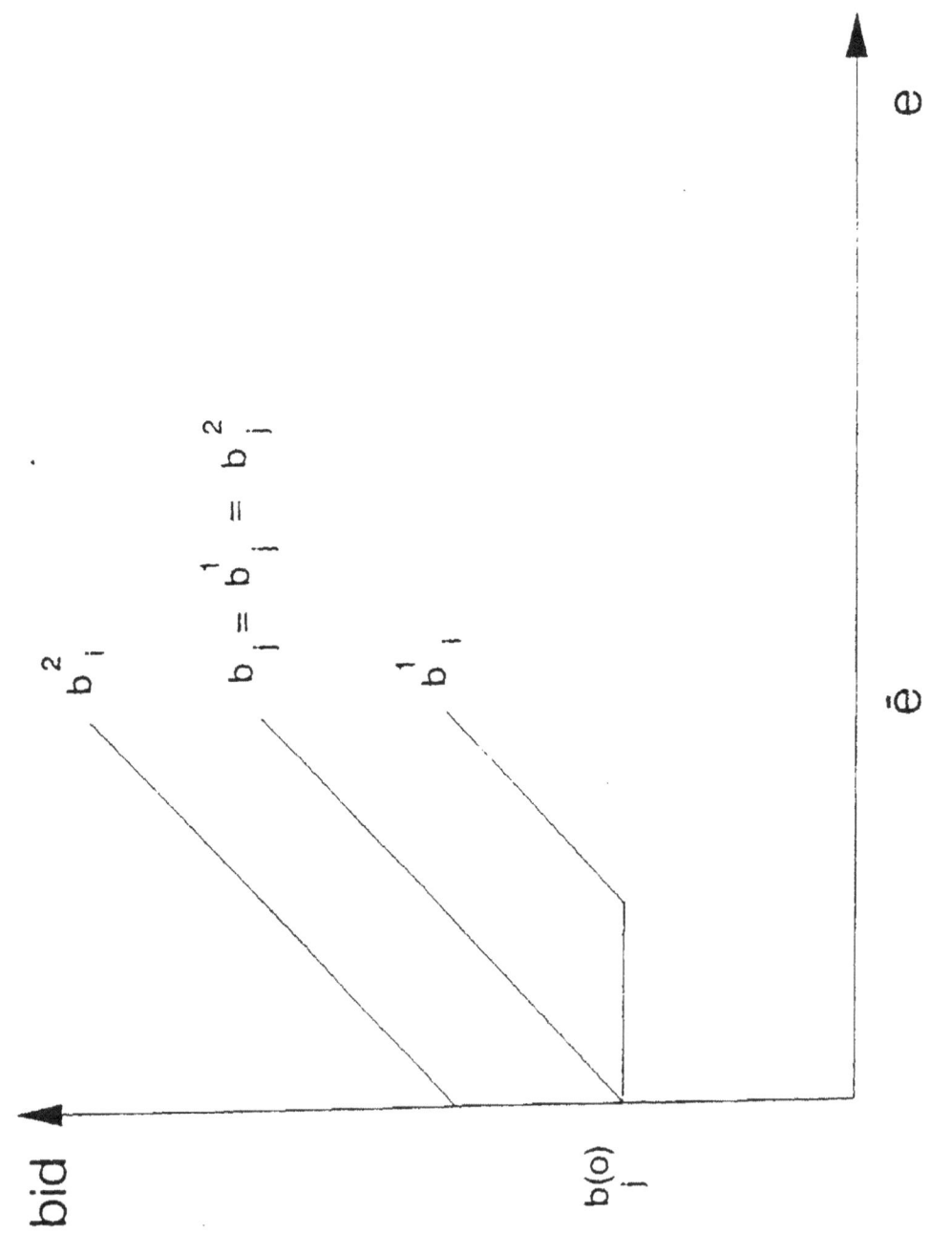

Equilibrium Bidding Functions

FIGURE 4

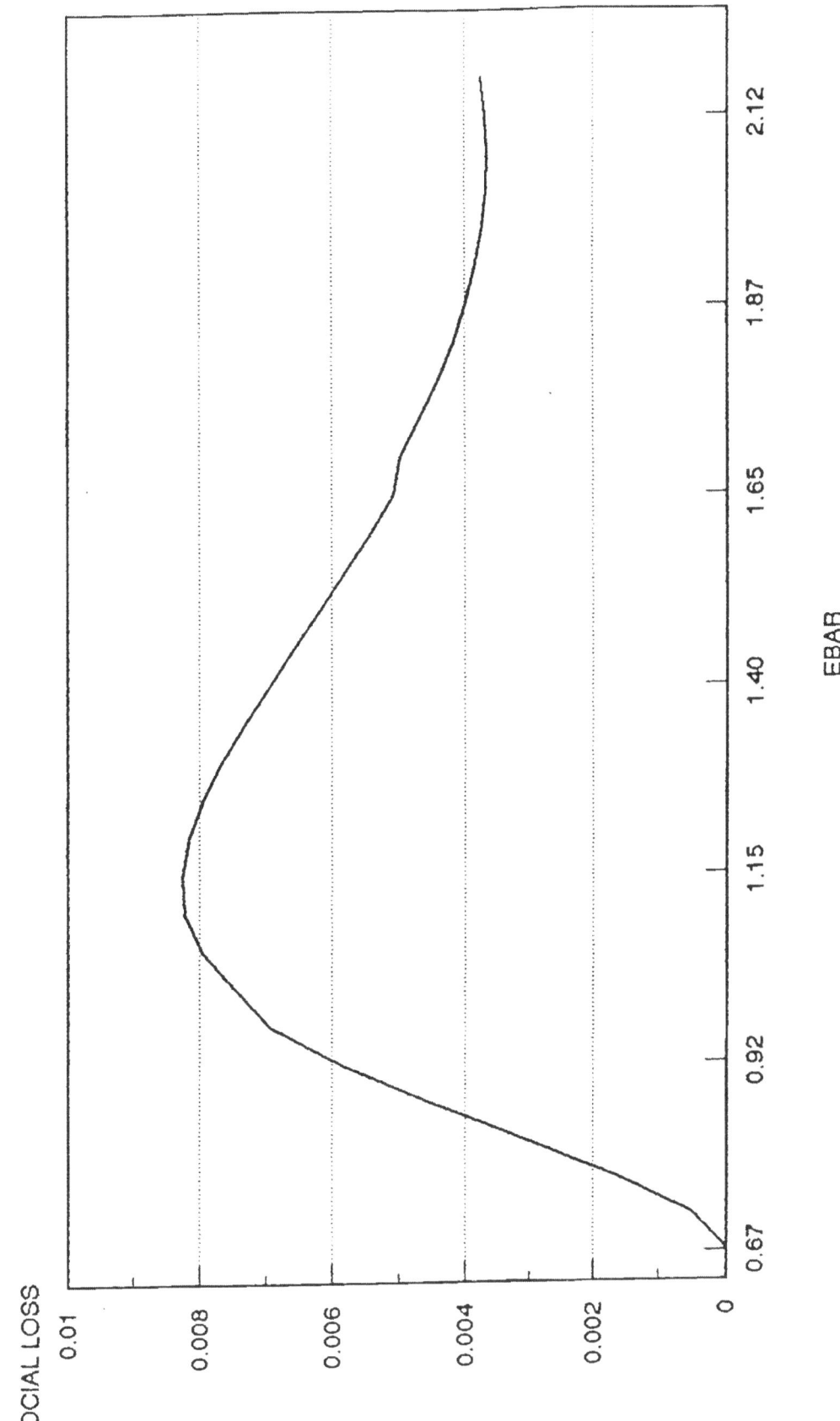

SOCIAL LOSS UNDER SEQUENTIAL AUCTION REGIME
WHEN DELTA C = 1

SOCIAL LOSS

EBAR

FIGURE 5

Social Loss Under Asymmetric Simultaneous
Auction Regime
When Delta C = 1

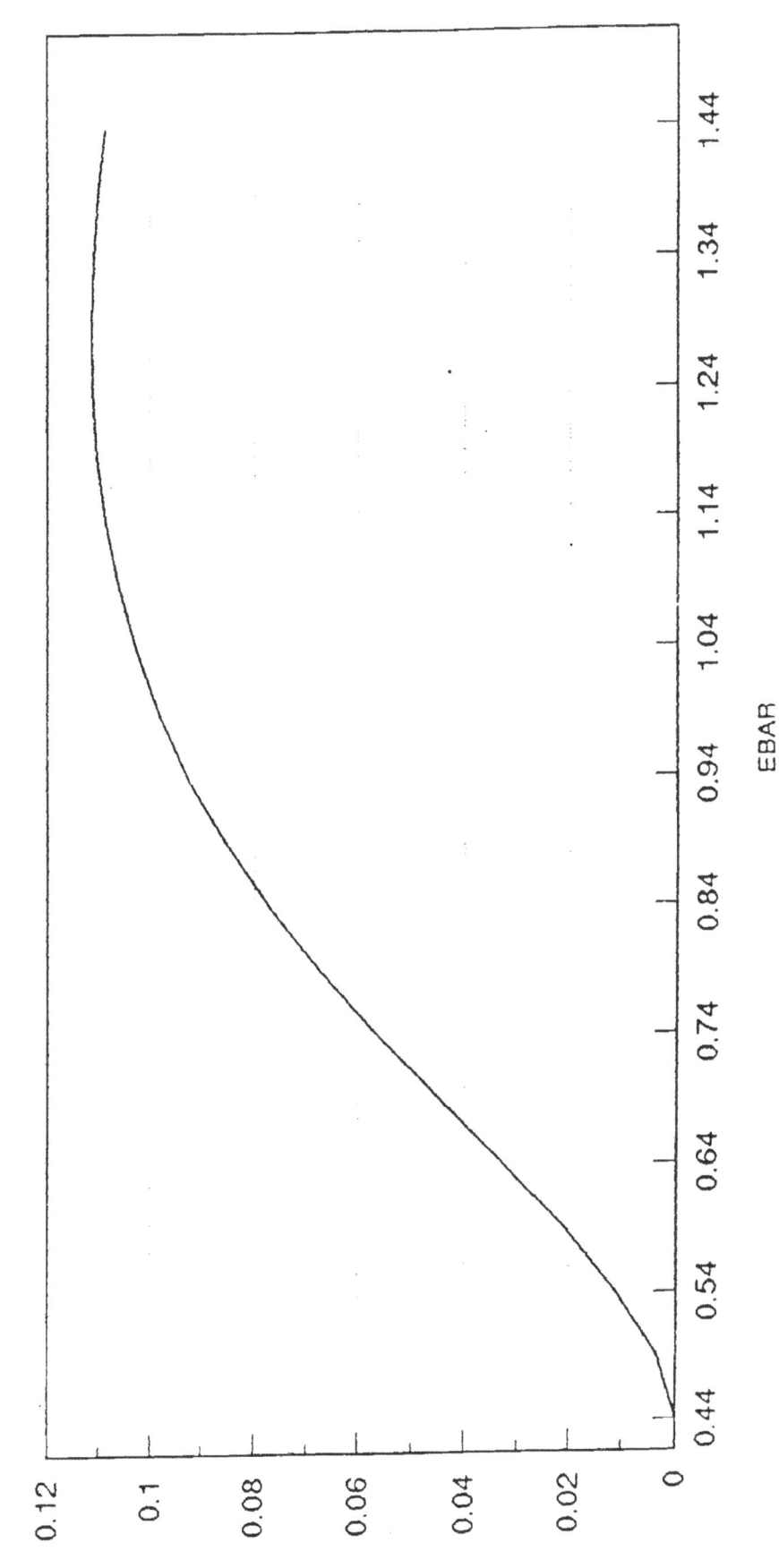

FIGURE 6

Difference Between Bid Prices Under Sequential and Simultaneous Auctions

Results in Sequential Auction	Results in Simultaneous Auction: $e_i < \Delta c/2 - \bar{e}/8$ — i wins both	j wins one	$e_i > \Delta c/2 - \bar{e}/8$ — j wins one / j wins both
i wins both	$\dfrac{\Delta c}{12} - \dfrac{5\bar{e}}{16} + \Gamma + \dfrac{e_i}{2}$	---	$\dfrac{\Delta c}{3} - \dfrac{3\bar{e}}{8} + \Gamma$
j wins one and $e_{min} < \dot{e}$ -& $e_{max} > \breve{e}$	$\dfrac{\Delta c}{12} - \dfrac{5\bar{e}}{16} + \Gamma$	$\Gamma + \dfrac{e_i}{2} + \dfrac{e_i}{4} - \dfrac{\bar{e}}{2}$	$\dfrac{\Delta c}{4} - \dfrac{9\bar{e}}{16} + \Gamma + \dfrac{e_i}{4}$
-& $e_{max} < \breve{e}$	$\dfrac{\Delta c}{12} - \dfrac{5\bar{e}}{16} + \Gamma$	$\Gamma + \dfrac{\Delta c}{3} + \dfrac{e_i}{2} - \dfrac{\bar{e}}{4} - \dfrac{e_i}{2}$	$\dfrac{7\Delta c}{12} - \dfrac{5\bar{e}}{16} + \Gamma - \dfrac{e_i}{2}$
j wins one and $\breve{e} > e_{min} > \dot{e}$	$\dfrac{7\Delta c}{36} - \dfrac{13\bar{e}}{48} + \dfrac{3e_i}{4} - \dfrac{3e_i}{2}$	$\dfrac{4\Delta c}{9} + \dfrac{\bar{e}}{3} + \dfrac{3e_{max} - e_{min}}{4} - \dfrac{e_i}{2}$	$\left\{\begin{array}{l} \dfrac{25\Delta c}{36} + \dfrac{25\bar{e}}{48} - \dfrac{3e_{min}}{2} \\[4pt] \dfrac{e_{max}}{4} - \dfrac{\bar{e}}{16} - \dfrac{5\Delta c}{12} + \dfrac{(\bar{e}-e_{min})\,\Delta c}{8\bar{e}} \\[4pt] \dfrac{2\Delta c^2}{9} + \dfrac{3(\bar{e}-e_{min})}{8\bar{e}} \end{array}\right.$
j wins one and $e_{min} > \breve{e}$	----	---	---
j wins both	----	---	$\dfrac{\Delta c}{3} - \dfrac{\bar{e}}{4} + \Gamma + \dfrac{e_i}{4}$

$$\text{where } \Gamma = \frac{2\Delta c^2}{9(\bar{e}-e_i)} + \frac{(\bar{e}-\breve{e})^2(3\bar{e}-2\Delta c)}{6(\bar{e}-e_i)^2} + \frac{\bar{e}\breve{e}-\breve{e}^2-\bar{e}e_i+e_i^2}{2(\bar{e}-e_i)}$$

Table 1

PROBABILITY THAT ONE
BIDDER WINS BOTH AUCTIONS

$\bar{e}$	ASYMMETRIC SIMULTANEOUS EQUILIBRIUM	SYMMETRIC SEQUENTIAL EQUILIBRIUM
0.47	1.6%	0.0%
0.52	1.6%	0.0%
0.57	2.4%	0.0%
0.62	4.3%	0.0%
0.67	6.9%	0.0%
0.72	9.7%	0.1%
0.77	12.7%	0.4%
0.82	15.6%	1.0%
0.87	18.5%	1.6%
0.92	21.3%	2.4%
0.97	24.0%	3.3%
1	26.6%	4.0%

$$(\Delta c = 1)$$

TABLE 2

COMPARISON OF EXPECTED SOCIAL LOSS
UNDER ALTERNATIVE AUCTION REGIMES

$\bar{e}$	SEQUENTIAL	SIMULTANEOUS ASYMMETRIC	SIMULTANEOUS SYMMETRIC
0.05	0.000	0.000	0.492
0.1	0.000	0.000	0.483
0.15	0.000	0.000	0.475
0.2	0.000	0.000	0.467
0.25	0.000	0.000	0.458
0.3	0.000	0.000	0.450
0.35	0.000	0.000	0.442
0.4	0.000	0.000	0.433
0.45	0.000	0.000	0.425
0.5	0.000	0.004	0.417
0.55	0.000	0.012	0.408
0.6	0.000	0.022	0.400
0.65	0.000	0.034	0.392
0.7	0.000	0.046	0.383
0.75	0.001	0.058	0.375
0.8	0.003	0.069	0.367
0.85	0.004	0.078	0.358
0.9	0.005	0.086	0.350
0.95	0.007	0.093	0.342
1	0.008	0.099	0.333
1.05	0.008	0.103	0.325
1.1	0.008	0.107	0.317
1.15	0.008	0.109	0.309
1.2	0.008	0.110	0.301
1.25	0.008	0.111	0.293
1.3	0.007	0.111	0.286

$(\Delta c = 1)$ TABLE 3